Understanding the
Passion
of Jesus
made easy

Mark Water

John Hunt
Publishing Limited

Copyright © 2004 John Hunt Publishing Ltd
Deershot Lodge, Park Lane, Ropley,
Hants, SO24 OBE, UK.
Tel: +44 (0) 1962 773768 Fax: +44 (0) 1962 773769
E-mail: office@johnhunt-publishing.com
www.johnhunt-publishing.com

Text: © 2004 Mark Water

Designed by Andrew Milne Design,
www.milnedesign.co.uk

ISBN 1 84298 155 2

Printed by South China Printing Co.,
Hong Kong/China

CONTENTS

WHAT DOES THE "PASSION" OF JESUS MEAN?

Dictionary definition

- The word "Passion" comes from a Latin word meaning "suffering."
  pas•sion \ pa-sh_n \ – noun.
- This is Middle English, from Old French, from Late Latin *passion, passio,* suffering, being acted upon, from Latin *pati* to suffer.

The sufferings of Jesus

- The Passion of Christ refers to the sufferings of Jesus between the night of the Last Supper, on Thursday evening, and his death on Friday afternoon. In Mel Gibson's film, *The Passion of the Christ,* the focus is on the last twelve hours of his life.

The crucial question: Why?

- The Gospels of Matthew, Mark, Luke, and John do not concentrate on the physical suffering of Jesus.
- The letters in the New Testament *explain* rather than *describe* the death of Jesus.
- The whole of the New Testament answers the following questions:
    - Why did Christ suffer?
    - Why did Christ die?
    - What did Jesus achieve through his suffering?
    - What was the significance of one man's death, on a hill called Calvary outside Jerusalem, for the whole world?
    - How does Jesus' Passion affect me?

QUOTE ABOUT
THE PASSION OF JESUS

*"I could never myself
believe in God, if it
were not for the cross . . .
In the real world of
pain, how could one
worship a God who was
immune to it?"*
JOHN STOTT

JESUS' DEATH: *THE* CENTRAL EVENT IN THE GOSPELS

Jesus' last week

- The Gospels allot a disproportionate amount of space to the last week of Jesus' life.
- Matthew, Mark, Luke, and John all spend a huge proportion of their Gospels recording the circumstances leading up to and surrounding Jesus' death, as well as the Passion of Jesus itself.

The Passion of Jesus in the Gospels

GOSPEL	Total no. of chs	No. of chs on the Passion	List of chs on the Passion	Chs on the Passion as a % of the Gospel
MATTHEW	28	7	21-27	25%
MARK	16	5	11-15	31%
LUKE	24	5	19-23	21%
JOHN	21	8	12-19	30%

Verses in the Gospels devoted to Jesus' last week

GOSPEL	Total no. of of verses in Gospel	No. of verses about Jesus' Passion	Verses on the the Passion as a % of Gospel
MATTHEW	1071	323	30%
MARK	678	233	34%
LUKE	1151	260	23%
JOHN	879	286	33%

- Out of the total number of verses in the four Gospels, 3779 verses, 1102 verses are about Jesus' Passion. In percentage terms, that is almost 30%, 29.16% to be exact.

QUOTE ABOUT
THE PASSION OF JESUS

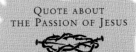

"I am telling the story as the Bible tells it. I think the story, as it really happened, speaks for itself. The Gospel is a complete script, and that's what we are filming."
MEL GIBSON, SPEAKING ABOUT *THE PASSION OF THE CHRIST*

EVENTS AT JESUS' CRUCIFIXION

Order of events

• If you combine the four accounts of Jesus' Passion from the Gospels of Matthew, Mark, Luke, and John you arrive at the following probable order of events of Jesus' execution.

1 Jesus arrives at Golgotha.
Matthew 27:33

2 Jesus declines to have his pain diminished with a drink of wine mixed with gall.
Matthew 27:34

3 Jesus is crucified between two thieves.
Luke 23:32-33

4 Jesus' first "word" from the cross.
Luke 23:34

5 The soldiers gamble for Jesus' clothes.
Luke 23:34

6 Passers-by laugh at Jesus.
Matthew 27:39-40

7 Jewish religious leaders make fun of Jesus.
Matthew 27:41-43

8 The rulers sneer at Jesus.
Luke 23:35

9 The soldiers mock Jesus.
Luke 23:36-37

10 The two thieves insult Jesus, but one repents.
Matthew 27:44; Luke 23:39-43

11 Jesus' second "word" from the cross.
Luke 23:43

12 Jesus' third "word" from the cross.
John 19:26

13 Three hours of darkness.
Luke 23:44-45

14 Jesus' fourth "word" from the cross.
Mark 15:34

15 Jesus' fifth "word" from the cross.
John 19:28

16 Jesus' sixth "word" from the cross.
John 19:30

17 Jesus' seventh "word" from the cross.
Luke 23:46

18 Jesus gives up his spirit.
Matthew 27:50

19 Jesus' side is pierced.
John 19:34

20 Jesus' body is taken down from the cross.
Matthew 27:57-61; John 19:38-42

9

QUOTE ABOUT THE PASSION OF JESUS

"You will never read the Bible again the same way. You won't come to these last chapters in the Gospels and read them the same way."
FRANKLIN GRAHAM
(AFTER VIEWING *THE PASSION OF THE CHRIST*)

Where is Jesus' death spoken about in the Old Testament?

The Lamb of God

- When John the Baptist saw Jesus coming toward him at the River Jordan he called him "the Lamb of God." "The next day John saw Jesus coming toward him and said, 'Look, the Lamb of God, who takes away the sin of the world!'" *John 1:29*

- Lambs were used as a Passover offering since the days of Moses.

Three echoes from the Old Testament

- The idea that Jesus is the "Lamb of God" takes up three themes from the Old Testament. They come from:
  - The lamb of the sin-offering
  - The Passover lamb
  - The suffering servant in Isaiah 53

- Jesus begins his ministry under the shadow of the cross. For it was on the cross that Jesus is seen as the "Lamb of God."

- Peter picks up this idea in his first letter, where he also pictures Jesus as the "Lamb of God" when he writes about "the precious blood of Christ, a lamb without blemish or defect." *1 Peter 1:19*

Quote about the Passion of Jesus

"Every time I preach or speak about the Cross, the things I saw on the screen [while I watched **The Passion of the Christ]** *will be on my heart and mind."*
Billy Graham

The Old Testament's sacrificial system

- Many pages of the Old Testament are full of details about God's instructions concerning animal sacrifices. Hebrews 9:23 states that Jesus' sacrifice was better than all these.

- Hebrews also compares Jesus' death, that is, his blood, with the death of animal sacrifices, in this way: "He [Christ] did not enter by means of the blood of goats and calves; but he entered the Most Holy Place once for all by his own blood, having obtained eternal redemption." *Hebrews 9:12*

Hebrews and Leviticus

- The New Testament letter of Hebrews is one long commentary on the Old Testament book of Leviticus.

- Hebrews explains how:
  - Jesus is the fulfillment of the ceremonial law
  - Christianity is superior to Judaism
  - Christ is better than anything that pointed to him

- The word "better" comes thirteen times in the letter to the Hebrews, showing how Jesus is the substance, and Judaism is the shadow.

Bible study

- A helpful way to study the Old Testament background to Jesus' death is to look up the cross-references to the book of Leviticus from the letter to the Hebrews.

- For example, Hebrews 10 is about Christ's once and for all sacrifice. The background to this comes in Leviticus 16:34: "'This is to be a lasting ordinance for you: Atonement is to be made once a year for all the sins of the Israelites.' And it was done, as the Lord commanded Moses."

- Hebrews 10:3, referring to the Old Testament sacrifices, states, "But those sacrifices are an annual reminder of sins."

JESUS' DEATH AND THE PSALMS

Psalm 22

- The death of Jesus is depicted most clearly in Psalm 22.
- The following six comparisons indicate how Psalm 22 is a divinely inspired prophecy about some of the details of the death of Jesus.

QUOTE ABOUT THE PASSION OF JESUS

"Can you imagine, a Psalmist a thousand years before it actually happened describing exactly what people are going to be saying to Jesus as he's hanging on the cross? It absolutely boggles your mind."
GORDON ROBERTSON ON PSALM 22 AND *THE PASSION OF THE CHRIST*

Theme	Verse/s in Psalm 22	Verses from the Gospels
1 Jesus is insulted	"But I am a worm and not a man, scorned by men and despised by the people. All who see me mock me; they hurl insults, shaking their heads." *Verses 6-7*	"In the same way the chief priests, the teachers of the law and the elders mocked him. 'He saved others,' they said, 'but he can't save himself! He's the King of Israel! Let him come down now from the cross, and we will believe in him. He trusts in God. Let God rescue him now if he wants him, for he said, "I am the Son of God."' In the same way the robbers who were crucified with him also heaped insults on him." *Matthew 27:41-44*
2 Crucified	Verses 13-15	Matthew 27:27
3 Stared at	"I can count all my bones; people stare and gloat over me." *Verse 17*	"And sitting down, they kept watch over him there." *Matthew 27:36*
4 Jesus' clothes divided up	"They divide my garments among them and cast lots for my clothing." *Verse 18*	"When they had crucified him, they divided up his clothes by casting lots." *Matthew 27:35*
5 Forsaken by God	Verse 1	Matthew 27:46
6 Pierced	"Dogs have surrounded me; a band of evil men has encircled me, they have pierced my hands and my feet." *Verse 16*	"Instead, one of the soldiers pierced Jesus' side with a spear, bringing a sudden flow of blood and water." *John 19:34*

HOW IS ISAIAH CHAPTER 53 LINKED TO JESUS' DEATH? (1)

Isaiah 52:13–53:12

- Isaiah 53, actually Isaiah 52:13–53:12, is probably the clearest and most detailed Old Testament prophecy about the Passion and death of Jesus.

Six links between the death of Jesus and Isaiah 53

Theme	Isaiah's prophecy	New Testament fulfillment
1 Jesus is despised and rejected	"He was despised and rejected by men, a man of sorrows, and familiar with suffering. Like one from whom men hide their faces he was despised, and we esteemed him not." *Isaiah 53:3*	Matthew 27:30-31; John 1:11
2 Healing by Jesus' wounds	". . . and by his wounds we are healed." *Isaiah 53:5*	"Then Pilate took Jesus and had him flogged." *John 19:1*
3 Jesus took our sins on himself	"But he was pierced for our transgressions, he was crushed for our iniquities; the punishment that brought us peace was upon him, . . ." *Isaiah 53:5*	1 Peter 2:24

4 Jesus did not accuse his persecutors	Isaiah 53:7	Matthew 27:11-14
5 Jesus took our sin on himself	"We all, like sheep, have gone astray, each of us has turned to his own way; and the LORD has laid on him the iniquity of us all." *Isaiah 53:6*	"He was delivered over to death for our sins and was raised to life for our justification." *Romans 4:25*
6 Jesus was judged	Isaiah 53:8	Matthew 27:11-26

Luther and the wounds of Jesus

"If you want to understand the Christian message you must start with the wounds of Christ." *Martin Luther*

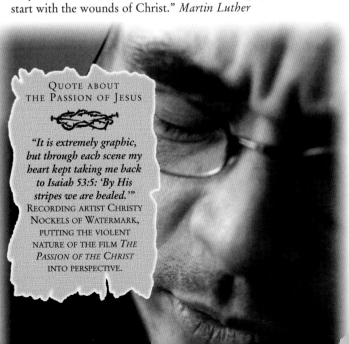

QUOTE ABOUT
THE PASSION OF JESUS

"It is extremely graphic, but through each scene my heart kept taking me back to Isaiah 53:5: 'By His stripes we are healed.'"
RECORDING ARTIST CHRISTY NOCKELS OF WATERMARK, PUTTING THE VIOLENT NATURE OF THE FILM THE PASSION OF THE CHRIST INTO PERSPECTIVE.

Isaiah 52 and 53 and the New Testament

- Every New Testament writer, except for Jude and James, quotes from Isaiah 52:1–53:12.

Theme	Isaiah's prophecy	New Testament fulfillment
7 Jesus was buried with the rich	"He was assigned a grave with the wicked, and with the rich in his death, though he had done no violence, nor was any deceit in his mouth." *Isaiah 53:9*	"As evening approached, there came a rich man from Arimathea, named Joseph, who had himself become a disciple of Jesus. Going to Pilate, he asked for Jesus' body, and Pilate ordered that it be given to him. Joseph took the body, wrapped it in a clean linen cloth, and placed it in his own new tomb that he had cut out of the rock. He rolled a big stone in front of the entrance to the tomb and went away." Matthew 27:57-60
8 Jesus was made sin for us	Isaiah 53:10	2 Corinthians 5:21

9 Jesus' righteousness brings justification	Isaiah 53:11	Romans 5:18
10 The death of Jesus	Isaiah 53:12	Romans 3:25
11 Jesus was numbered with the transgressors	Isaiah 53:12	Mark 15:28
12 Jesus prayed for the transgressors	"Therefore I will give him a portion among the great, and he will divide the spoils with the strong,because he poured out his life unto death, and was numbered with the transgressors. For he bore the sin of many, and made intercession for the transgressors." *Isaiah 53:12*	"Jesus said, 'Father, forgive them, for they do not know what they are doing.'" *Luke 23:34*

QUOTE ABOUT THE PASSION OF JESUS

"The suffering of Jesus Christ was foretold by Isaiah the prophet. A sinless one would come. He would be beaten beyond recognition. But the sins of all of us – our iniquities, our sicknesses, and our diseases were laid on Him, and it pleased Jehovah God to bruise Him. It wasn't the Jews. It wasn't the Romans. It wasn't anybody. It was God Himself that brought this about. Why? So that you and I could know salvation."
PAT ROBERTSON ON ISAIAH 53

WAS JESUS TAKEN BY SURPRISE?

Wrong ideas

- Many wrong ideas about the death have circulated over the centuries, and they keep on raising their heads from time to time.

1 Circumstances forced Jesus to be crucified

- Nothing could be further from the truth.
- Before Jesus decided to enter Jerusalem publicly, humbly riding on a donkey, he deliberately kept a low profile. "Therefore Jesus no longer moved about publicly among the Jews. Instead he withdrew to a region near the desert, to a village called Ephraim, where he stayed with his disciples." *John 11:54*

- When Jesus went up to Jerusalem, he knew he would be arrested and crucified. He was totally in control of events. Events did not dictate what happened to him.

2 Jesus had a death-wish

- Today some suicide bombers gladly go to their death, being blown up into a thousand pieces. But Jesus was not like them. Jesus' death was not really a martyrdom. In one sense Jesus did not "long to be crucified." This is clear from Jesus' prayer in the Garden of Gethsemane. "Father, if you are willing, take this cup from me; yet not my will, but yours be done." *Luke 22:42*

QUOTE ABOUT
THE PASSION OF JESUS

"My hope is that this movie will affect people on a very profound level and reach them with a message of faith, hope, love, and forgiveness."
MEL GIBSON, SPEAKING ABOUT *THE PASSION OF THE CHRIST*

Jesus often predicted his own death

"From that time on Jesus began to explain to his disciples that he must go to Jerusalem and suffer many things at the hands of the elders, chief priests and teachers of the law, and that he must be killed and on the third day be raised to life."
Matthew 16:21

- See also Mark 8:31–9:1; Luke 9:22-27; and Matthew 20:17-29; Mark 10:32-34; Luke 18:31-33.

So, why was Jesus prepared to die?

- Central to the Christian gospel is the concept of Jesus' active obedience.
- Jesus not only died on the cross, for the sins of his sheep but he established their righteousness through his perfect obedience to God's Law.
- When Jesus died on the cross, he did so in perfect obedience to the Father's will.

Who killed Jesus? (1) Wasn't Pontius Pilate to blame?

Who is to blame?

- Humanly speaking, we can say that a number of people were responsible for Jesus' death:
  - Judas Iscariot, for betraying Jesus
  - The Jewish high priests, for condemning Jesus
  - Pontius Pilate, for allowing the crucifixion to proceed
  - The crowd, for baying for Jesus' blood
  - The Roman soldiers, for driving in the nails

Pontius Pilate

- The Jewish authorities did not love Pontius Pilate, as he stood for the might and power of Rome and the occupying force in their beloved country.
- But the Jews had a problem. Only the Romans were allowed to impose the death penalty on a prisoner. So the Jews took Jesus to Pilate.
- Pilate himself knew that Jesus was innocent. Mark 15:10 records that Pilate knew that, "it was out of envy that the chief priests had handed Jesus over to him."
- When the angry crowd shouted at Pilate, "Crucify him [Jesus]" he countered them by asking: "Why? What crime has he committed?" *Mark 15:14*
- But, Pilate can hardly be thought of as being innocent of Jesus' death: "Wanting to satisfy the crowd, Pilate released Barabbas to them. He had Jesus flogged, and handed him over to be crucified." *Mark 15:15*

What about Pilate's wife?

- There is only one thing recorded in the Gospels about Pilate's wife: her dream.
  "While Pilate was sitting on the judge's seat, his wife sent him this message: 'Don't have anything to do with that innocent man, for I have suffered a great deal today in a dream because of him.'" *Matthew 27:19*

- In the film *The Passion of the Christ*, Pilate's wife brings linen strips to Jesus' mother and Mary Magdalene so that they can wipe up his body. But there is no hint of this in the four Gospels.

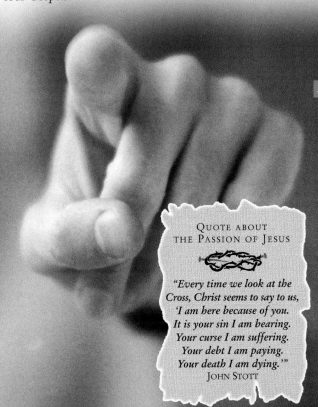

QUOTE ABOUT
THE PASSION OF JESUS

"Every time we look at the Cross, Christ seems to say to us, 'I am here because of you. It is your sin I am bearing. Your curse I am suffering. Your debt I am paying. Your death I am dying.'"
JOHN STOTT

WHO KILLED JESUS? (2)
WASN'T IT ROMAN SOLDIERS?

The Gospel record

- The Roman soldiers had to obey orders. If they were on crucifixion duty their job was to undertake the gruesome procedure of this barbaric and excruciatingly painful form of execution. But mocking the condemned man was not part of their job description.

The soldiers mock Jesus

"Then the governor's soldiers took Jesus into the Praetorium and gathered the whole company of soldiers round him. They stripped him and put a scarlet robe on him, and then wove a crown of thorns and set it on his head. They put a staff in his right hand and knelt in

front of him and mocked him. 'Hail, King of the Jews!' they said. They spat on him, and took the staff and struck him on the head again and again. After they had mocked him, they took off the robe and put his own clothes on him. Then they led him away to crucify him."
Matthew 27:27-31

"Complaints that the Gospels are more sparing in the description of Christ's sufferings are accurate but miss the point. Then people could fill in the meaning of 'cross' from their own culture. We need a film like this to drive it home to us."
DR. MARK BONNINGTON,
ST. JOHN'S COLLEGE,
DURHAM UNIVERSITY,
SPEAKING ABOUT *THE
PASSION OF THE CHRIST*

Is *The Passion of the Christ* too violent?

- Some critics and reviewers have asked: Who would want to see a film this violent? For it shows whippings, floggings, and the Crucifixion, in close-up with many slow motion shots. It leaves nothing to the imagination, showing a cat-o-nine tails rip repeatedly into Jesus' body, which is seen as a bleeding pulp.

- Other commentators saw the violent aspect of the film differently. "John's simple words, 'But he [Pilate] had Jesus flogged, Matthew 27:26, feel vastly different as you watch two brutal Roman soldiers go on minute after terrible minute bludgeoning Jesus' near-naked body with flesh-gouging whips. Pious talk about Jesus' death for our sins takes on a whole new meaning." *Ron Sider, President, Evangelicals For Social Action*

Arrest and Trial

The plot

After Jesus brought Lazarus back from the dead, "the chief priests and the Pharisees called a meeting of the Sanhedrin," and "from that day on they plotted to take his life." *John 11:47,53*

The arrest

Judas guided "some officials from the chief priests and Pharisees," John 18:3, to arrest Jesus.

From Caiaphas to Pilate

"Then the Jews led Jesus from Caiaphas to the palace of the Roman governor." *John 18:28*

Whipping up the crowd

"But the chief priests and the elders persuaded the crowd to ask for Barabbas and to have Jesus executed." *Matthew 27:20*

Mel Gibson's hand

- Mel Gibson's left hand makes a cameo appearance in his movie. In the crucifixion scene, Gibson holds the first nail that is driven into Jesus' hand. We are being told that each and every one of us is responsible for Jesus' death. Gibson is convinced that we all had a hand in causing Jesus' suffering and death.

Never forget

- Jesus died because each one of us is a sinner. None of us can escape responsibility for Jesus' death.

QUOTE ABOUT THE PASSION OF JESUS

"Who killed Jesus Christ? The big answer is that we all did. I'll be first in the culpability stakes. Jesus Christ was crucified for all men of all creeds for all time. And he died for all of us."
MEL GIBSON

JESUS HIMSELF SPEAKS ABOUT HIS PASSION

Jesus predicted his crucifixion

- Jesus often taught his disciples that he was born to die.
- When Jesus predicted his own death he said that this would include:
  - Suffering
  - Rejection
  - Being killed

"He [Jesus] then began to teach them that the Son of Man must suffer many things and be rejected by the elders, chief priests and teachers of the law, and that he must be killed and after three days rise again." *Mark 8:31*

"Oh no you don't"

- When the apostle Peter was told by Jesus that he would be killed, "Peter took him aside and began to rebuke him" *Mark 8:32*. Peter could not stand the idea that Jesus should be killed. But Peter was completely missing the whole point of Jesus' mission.

"Oh yes I do"

- Jesus told Peter off in the strongest possible terms for his rebuke. He even called Peter "Satan": "But when Jesus turned and looked at his disciples, he rebuked Peter. 'Out of my sight, Satan!' he said. 'You do not have in mind the things of God, but the things of men.'" *Mark 8:33*

A first-century execution

- Jesus may never have emphasized the terrible physical suffering of his own crucifixion, but the people of his day would have been horrified at the thought of this, in a way that we can only imagine. They knew, at first hand, what was involved in this cruel form of Roman execution.

"The great strength of
The Passion of the
Christ is that it helps us
realize just how
sanitized the words
'cross' and 'crucifixion'
have become after 2000
years. Familiarity has
robbed these words of
much of their impact. In
a society that regards
public execution as
primitive, distasteful,
and even immoral, we
no longer hear with first
century ears. That Jesus
not merely died but was
subjected to the
deliberately cruel and
degrading death of a
criminal really comes
home in the film."
DR. MARK BONNINGTON, ST.
JOHN'S COLLEGE, DURHAM
UNIVERSITY

DETAILS OF A ROMAN CRUCIFIXION

Capital punishment
- Roman crucifixion, one of the most painful deaths ever devised, was reserved by the Romans as the death penalty for convicted criminals.
- The torture lasted many hours, and sometimes even days.

The cross
- The most widely used cross had two parts, made of two pieces of wood.

Stipes

The upright piece of wood, known as the *stipes*, was a permanent fixture and remained in place in the ground, before and after a crucifixion.

Patibulum

The second piece of wood, the crosspiece, known as the *patibulum*, was hauled to the place of execution by the condemned criminal.

"Carrying his own cross, he [Jesus] went out to The Place of the Skull." *John 19:17*

But the *patibulum* weighed as much as 300 pounds and so a recently flogged man would not have had the strength to carry it himself. "As they were going out, they met a man from Cyrene, named Simon, and they forced him to carry the cross." *Matthew 27:32*

Archaeological discoveries

- In 1968 the bones of a Jew who had been crucified in Jerusalem at the time of Jesus was discovered. It shows how Jesus' body would have been fixed to the cross. An inscription identified the crucified victim as "Jehohannan Ben" (son of Jehohannan).

- A rough nail (iron spike) about six inches long was driven into each wrist, not into the palms of the hands, which would have torn under the weight of the body.

- A single spike was used to attach Jesus' feet to the cross. His toes and heels were put together and then turned so that they lay sideways on the cross. A board was placed over them before the third spike was driven through the board and both of his heels.

- John, in his Gospel, simply refers to all of the above with the words, "Here [at Golgotha] they crucified him." *John 19:18*

QUOTE ABOUT
THE PASSION OF JESUS

"The Passion of the Christ *is emotionally wrenching because it is brutally honest about the violence of Jesus' death. Never in my life have I seen any movie that comes even close to depicting what Roman crucifixion was really like. Long familiarity and theological explanation have leached out in our minds the awful brutality of Jesus' trial and death."*
RON SIDER, PRESIDENT, EVANGELICALS FOR SOCIAL ACTION

How did Jesus die?

Was it by suffocating?

- The body of a criminal lay in an agonizingly contorted position throughout the crucifixion. He could manage to breathe in relatively easily but had great problems in breathing out, as he was not in a position to naturally relax the muscles of the rib cage. So to breathe out he had to use his legs to slightly raise himself upwards. As soon as he could not do this he would die of suffocation.

Breaking legs

- Some people lasted for over twenty-four hours as they fought for their next breath. Some even survived for two days.

- The Jews had a problem with Jesus being crucified on the eve of the Feast of Unleavened Bread.
"Now it was the day of Preparation, and the next day was to be a special Sabbath. Because the Jews did not want the bodies left on the crosses during the Sabbath, they asked Pilate to have the legs broken and the bodies taken down."
John 19:31

- As a method of speeding up the end of a crucifixion the victim's legs were broken. The meant that their legs could no longer be used to raise themselves up and so they quickly died. So the soldiers broke the legs of the criminals on either side of Jesus, but were surprised to find that when they came to do the same to Jesus that he was already dead.

"The soldiers therefore came and broke the legs of the first man who had been crucified with Jesus, and then those of the other. But when they came to Jesus and found that he was already dead, they did not break his legs."
John 19:32-33

QUOTE ABOUT
THE PASSION OF JESUS

"Speaking personally, I was deeply affected by a single thought while watching the movie: I did this to Jesus."
JAMES DOBSON, SPEAKING ABOUT *THE PASSION OF THE CHRIST*

THE SOLDIER'S SPEAR

"When he had received the drink, Jesus said, "It is finished." With that, he bowed his head and gave up his spirit.

"Now it was the day of Preparation, and the next day was to be a special Sabbath. Because the Jews did not want the bodies left on the crosses during the Sabbath, they asked Pilate to have the legs broken and the bodies taken down. . . . But when they came to Jesus and found that he was already dead, they did not break his legs. Instead, one of the soldiers pierced Jesus' side with a spear, bringing a sudden flow of blood and water."
John 19:30-34

Postmortem

If it were possible to perform a postmortem on the body of Jesus, would we discover the time and cause of his death?

A strange observation

- John records one of the most puzzling aspects of Jesus' death: "one of the soldiers pierced Jesus' side with a spear, bringing a sudden flow of blood and water." *John 19:34*
- The mystery here is that dead men don't normally bleed in the manner described here, as they have no blood pressure.

The theologian's approach

- "Jesus called out with a loud voice, 'Father, into your hands I commit my spirit.' When he had said this, he breathed his last." *Luke 23:46*
  - "He gave up His life because He willed it, when He willed it, and as He willed it."
  St. Augustine

The medical approach

- The pericardium is a closed sac encasing the heart and lubricated by about a teaspoonful of fluid. But the pericardial fluid is increased to about twenty-four teaspoons (100ml) when the agony of death is prolonged. Doctors state that the pericardial cavity of a dead person contains about 500ml of fluid and newly clotted blood.

- So the water observed by John was most probably the watery fluid from the pericardium.

- The flowing action of the water and blood could lead one to believe that Christ was dead at the time he was stabbed by the soldier's spear.

- The blood that John saw was probably leaking form the torn wall of the heart of Jesus.

Jesus remained in control

- Jesus' death cannot be attributed to any mere physical cause. Jesus only died when he was ready to die. See John 10:17-18.

- Jesus did not have his life taken from him. He yielded it up when he chose to. See Luke 23:46. Matthew says that Jesus "gave up his spirit" *Matthew 27:50*. And John says that "When he had received the drink, Jesus said, 'It is finished.' With that, he bowed his head and gave up his spirit." *John 19:30*

QUOTE ABOUT
THE PASSION OF JESUS

"The Passion of the Christ *is one of the most amazing images of the real account of the crucifixion. What struck me most was the gritty, in-your-face account of the ultimate hero Jesus Christ."*
BRIAN BLOMBERG,
PROMISE KEEPERS

Jesus' Passion was a Ransom

Definition of "ransom"
- The word "ransom" means a deliverance from slavery by the payment of a price, which was often money or gold.

Hymn-writers' theme
- Popular hymns, like the one by Henry F. Lyte, often refer to Jesus as our ransom.

  "Praise, my soul, the King of Heaven;
  To His feet thy tribute bring.
  Ransomed, healed, restored, forgiven, . . . "

Jesus' death was a ransom
- According to both Matthew and Mark Jesus died to ransom us:
  ". . . the Son of Man did not come to be served, but to serve, and to give his life as a ransom for many." *Matthew 20:28*
  "For even the Son of Man did not come to be served, but to serve, and to give his life as a ransom for many." *Mark 10:45*

"God, in his infinite mercy, having determined to redeem us, became himself our Redeemer in the person of his only begotten Son."

JOHN CALVIN, THE INSTITUTES OF CHRISTIAN RELIGION

35

An image from slavery

- This idea about a "ransom" comes from the slave market. A young man is chained up, then someone comes along and pays money to the slave-owner. The slave's chains are then struck off and he becomes a free person.

- Through Jesus' death on the cross, say Matthew and Mark, Jesus provided the ransom price for our sin.

Jesus' Passion and the Last Supper

Jesus explains

- One of the clearest ways to understand the suffering and death of Jesus is to turn to what Jesus himself said on this subject.

The meal

- Jesus laid careful plans for the last meeting he would have with all his twelve disciples. Jesus had a meal with his closest friends. But it was no ordinary meal. What we now call the "Last Supper" was closely linked to the Jewish Passover. "And he said to them, 'I have eagerly desired to eat this Passover with you before I suffer.'" *Luke 22:15*

The Lord's Supper

- Jesus instituted the Lord's Supper to be a reminder of the central importance of his death.
- Jesus explained that his death would be a sacrifice for his people. Jesus was to shed his blood in a unique way. Jesus would die in a way that no other person could die.
- Jesus' death would provide spiritual benefits for all his present and future followers.

The broken bread

"While they were eating, Jesus took bread, gave thanks and broke it, and gave it to his disciples, saying, 'Take and eat; this is my body.'" *Matthew 26:26*

- The breaking of the bread indicated what would happen to Jesus' body. This symbolic act is explained by Paul. He says that Jesus' body was "broken for you."
  "And when he had given thanks, he brake it, and said, Take, eat: this is my body, which is broken for you: this do in remembrance of me." *1 Corinthians 11:24 KJV*

The poured-out wine

- The meaning of Jesus' death is brought out again very clearly in the symbolic act Jesus made with the cup of wine at the Last Supper.

- Offering it to his disciples, he, "took the cup, gave thanks and offered it to them, saying, 'Drink from it, all of you. This is my blood of the covenant, which is poured out for many for the forgiveness of sins.'" *Matthew 26:27-28*

- The "blood" here refers to the death that results from blood being poured out in a sacrifice. This is the sense in which Jesus life was "poured out" for us.

- The whole purpose of the Passion of Jesus is here summarized in the words of Jesus himself: "for the forgiveness of sins."

QUOTE ABOUT
THE PASSION OF JESUS

"The Lord's Supper is an ordinance of Jesus Christ, to be administered with the elements of bread and wine, and to be observed by his churches till the end of the world. It is in no sense a sacrifice, but is designed to commemorate his death, to confirm the faith and other graces of Christians, and to be a bond, pledge, and renewal of their communion with him, and of their church fellowship."
SOUTHERN BAPTIST THEOLOGICAL SEMINARY

JESUS' SEVEN LAST "WORDS"

Love and authority

- The suffering of Jesus revealed his love for us. The seven "words" which he spoke from the cross reflect this.

First "word"

Jesus spoke to his Father as he was nailed to the cross. "Jesus said, 'Father, forgive them, for they do not know what they are doing.'"
Luke 23:34

Second "word"

Jesus spoke to the thief who was being crucified next to him.

"Jesus answered him, 'I tell you the truth, today you will be with me in paradise.'"
Luke 23:43

The repentant thief

- One of the thieves who was crucified with Jesus repented and asked Jesus to remember him when he came into his kingdom. Far from rebuking this man, Jesus promised him that he would be with him in the next life.

- It was amazing that this thief should perceive God's kingdom in the person of the dying Jesus.

The unrepentant thief

- Only one thief repented. The other kept on hurling abuse at Jesus.
  "One of the criminals who hung there hurled insults at him: 'Aren't you the Christ? Save yourself and us!'"
  Luke 23:39

- In *The Passion of the Christ*, a huge raven flies down, lands on the unrepentant criminal's crossbeam, and pecks his eye out. There is no hint in any of the Gospels that this ever happened.

Third "word"

Jesus spoke to his mother Mary and his disciple John who were standing together nearby.

To his mother, Jesus said, "'Dear woman, here is your son,' and to the disciple, 'Here is your mother.' From that time on, this disciple took her into his home." *John 19:26-27*

Fourth "word"

"About the ninth hour Jesus cried out in a loud voice, 'Eloi, Eloi, lama sabachthani?' – which means, 'My God, my God, why have you forsaken me?'" *Matthew 27:46*

Fifth "word"

"Later, knowing that all was now completed, and so that the Scripture would be fulfilled, Jesus said, 'I am thirsty.'" *John 19:28*

Sixth "word"

The sixth word was a statement of triumph. Jesus had completed his mission. "It is finished." *John 19:30*

Seventh "word"

"Jesus called out with a loud voice, 'Father, into your hands I commit my spirit.' When he had said this, he breathed his last." *Luke 23:46*

QUOTE ABOUT THE PASSION OF JESUS

"No crucified man, dying in agony, ever spoke like this. This was the voice of one who decides where thieves spend eternity."
JOHN PIPER

JESUS IS LIFTED UP ON THE CROSS

Jesus' death and lifting up

- In John's Gospel a strange, but highly significant, phrase is used in connection with the death of Jesus. Three times, John talks about Jesus being "lifted up."
- This points to:
    - The manner of Jesus' death (crucifixion)
    - Jesus' ultimate victory over sin and death

The first mention of "lifting up"

"'Just as Moses *lifted up* the snake in the desert, so the Son of Man must be *lifted up*, that everyone who believes in him may have eternal life.'"
John 3:14-15

- These verses show how John teaches about the necessity of Jesus' death. The Son of Man *must* be lifted up.

QUOTE ABOUT
THE PASSION OF JESUS

"There is no health of soul, nor hope of eternal life, except in the cross."
THOMAS À KEMPIS

The second mention of "lifting up"

"So Jesus said, 'When you have *lifted up* the Son of Man, then you will know who I am and that I do nothing on my own but speak just what the Father has taught me.'" *John 8:28*

- Lifting up is again seen to refer to Jesus' death. What might appear to be a tragedy to an onlooker, Jesus states will be a moment of revelation. It will show who he is. That God is his Father. That he is the Son of God.

The third mention of "lifting up"

"'But I, when I am *lifted up* from the earth, will draw all men to myself.' He said this to show the kind of death he was going to die." *John 12:32-33*

- This verse actually states that the phrase "lifted up" refers to "the kind of death he [Jesus] was going to die."

- The effect of Jesus' death is taught in this instance of "lifting up." Jesus will attract people to himself. The death of Jesus was never meant to be seen as being repulsive. The cross shows the spiritually magnetic power of Jesus.

- It is significant to note who Jesus was speaking to when he originally said these words. He was responding to an inquiry from "some Greeks," *John 12:20*.

- The point here is that when Jesus says that he will "draw *all* men" he means that his salvation is being made available to all types of people. Jesus came to save, not only the Jews, but non-Jews, the Greeks. All races are included in Jesus plan of salvation.

JESUS' PASSION WAS A SACRIFICE

Paul and the image of sacrifice

• Paul often connected the sacrifice of Jesus on the cross
with the lambs that were sacrificed for the Passover feast.
"For Christ, our Passover lamb, has been sacrificed."
1 Corinthians 5:7

Jesus' death and slain lambs

• There are a number of similarities between Jesus' death and
slain sacrificial lambs:

1 Lambs were used as a Passover offering since the days
of Moses.

2 Pilate pronounced his death sentence on Jesus at noon
on the Day of Preparation. Passover lambs were
slaughtered at noon on the Day of Preparation.
So Jesus died at the
same time that the
paschal lambs were
being slain in the
Temple in Jerusalem.

3 Jesus had no broken
bones when he died.
Passover lambs were
slaughtered in such a
way as not to break
any bones.

4 As a result of the
flogging Jesus received
and through the spear
thrown into his side,
you could say that
Jesus was drained of
blood. Passover Lambs
were drained of blood.

QUOTE ABOUT
THE PASSION OF JESUS

"*The lasting image [from
The Passion of the Christ] is
of blood, blood flowing, blood
flowing everywhere as Christ's
body is lacerated and crucified.
It is a visual presentation of
Isaac Watts' words: 'His dying
crimson like a robe, flows o'er
his body on the tree.'*"
DR. MARK BONNINGTON, ST.
JOHN'S COLLEGE, DURHAM
UNIVERSITY

"A fragrant offering"

- In a verse from his letter to the Ephesians Paul specifically identifies Jesus' self-giving as a sacrifice.
  "Christ loved us and gave himself up for us as a fragrant offering and sacrifice to God." *Ephesians 5:2*

- We note here that Jesus' sacrifice was rooted in love. The often-heard idea that Jesus' sacrifice somehow placated an angry God is found nowhere in the New Testament.

THE FIRST RESULT OF JESUS' PASSION

What happened as Jesus died?

- It is very interesting to note the first thing that happened after Jesus died. According to Matthew a strange and remarkable event took place in the Temple in Jerusalem.

Torn in two

- Jesus ended his human life with a cry of triumph, "It is finished." Jesus' mission had been successfully completed. He then committed his spirit to his Father. Matthew immediately explains what the crucifixion means, by telling us what else happened in Jerusalem "at that moment."
"And when Jesus had cried out again in a loud voice, he gave up his spirit. At that moment the curtain of the temple was torn in two from top to bottom."
Matthew 27:50-51

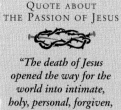

QUOTE ABOUT
THE PASSION OF JESUS

"The death of Jesus opened the way for the world into intimate, holy, personal, forgiven, joyful fellowship with God."
JOHN PIPER

A symbolic tearing

- In the Jerusalem Temple there was an inmost room, the most holy place. Nobody was allowed in there, except the high priest. And he was only allowed to go in there once a year in order to meet with the Lord.
- When Jesus was crucified, at the moment of his death, the huge curtain that separated the most holy place from the rest of the Temple was torn in two from top to bottom.

The meaning of the torn curtain

- The torn curtain meant that as Jesus' body was torn when he died, so God tore down the curtain that separated us all from himself.
- Jesus now provides us with direct access to God.

The letter to the Hebrews

- The letter to the Hebrews gives explanation after explanation about the sacrifice of Jesus. It speaks about our being able to enter the most holy place in the temple.
  "Therefore, brothers, since we have confidence to enter the Most Holy Place by the blood of Jesus, by a new and living way opened for us through the curtain, that is, his body, and since we have a great priest over the house of God, let us draw near to God with a sincere heart in full assurance of faith, having our hearts sprinkled to cleanse us from a guilty conscience and having our bodies washed with pure water."
  Hebrews 10:19-22
- Here the "curtain" is likened to Jesus' "body." As we can pass into a room when the curtain is drawn back, so we can pass into God's presence through the "blood," that is, through the death of Jesus.

JESUS IS A SUBSTITUTE FOR US

Sin for us

- The apostle Paul spells out his teaching most clearly, about Jesus being our substitute, in 2 Corinthians 5:21: "God made him who had no sin to be sin for us, so that in him we might become the righteousness of God."

The Old Testament background

- Paul, as a former Jew and leading rabbi, would have been very familiar with the Old Testament teaching about substitution.
- He was brought up with the symbolism of a goat being a scapegoat on the Day of Atonement. He knew that hands were placed on the scapegoat to symbolize the placing of the sins of the people onto the animal, before it was driven out into the wilderness.

The substitute idea

- The point about Jesus dying as our substitute is that he died on our behalf.
- We would have clearly understood this if we had been in Barabbas' shoes. Barabbas knew that he was justly condemned to death for all his criminal acts. Jesus was totally innocent of committing any crime. Jesus deserved to be freed; Barabbas deserved to die. But Jesus was condemned to die and "[Pilate] released Barabbas to them" *Matthew 27:26.* Barabbas must have felt that Jesus had died in his place.

Jesus died on our behalf

- Paul often wrote about how Jesus took our place when he died on the cross.
    - "He who did not spare his own Son, but gave him up for us all." *Romans 8:32*
    - "And he died for all." *2 Corinthians 5:15*
    - "Christ redeemed us from the curse of the law by becoming a curse for us, for it is written: 'Cursed is everyone who is hung on a tree.'" *Galatians 3:13*
    - "He died for us so that, whether we are awake or asleep, we may live together with him." *1 Thessalonians 5:10*

For us

- Note the way Paul underlines how Jesus died in our place, by observing how he repeats the phrases "For us," and "For us all."

QUOTE ABOUT
THE PASSION OF JESUS

"If Jesus Christ be God and died for me, then no sacrifice can be too great for me to make for him."
C. T. STUDD, FAMOUS CRICKETER AND PIONEER MISSIONARY

PAUL AND REDEMPTION

Paul explains Jesus' death

- Paul once wrote, "we preach Christ crucified"
  1 Corinthians 1:23. Paul spent his Christian life preaching
  about Jesus' death (and resurrection) and explaining the
  significance of these events.

Redemption

- One of Paul's favorite ways of teaching about the meaning
  behind the Passion of Jesus was by using the word
  "redemption." This word appears ten times in the New
  Testament, and it is used seven times by Paul.
  "... and are justified freely by his grace through the
  redemption that came by Christ Jesus." *Romans 3:24*
  "In him we have redemption through his blood, the
  forgiveness of sins." *Ephesians 1:7*

Redemption and the cross

- Paul links our redemption with the cross of Jesus. He says
  our redemption comes about "through his blood." Wherever
  the word "blood" is used in the New Testament letters in
  connection with Jesus, it always refers to his death. We are
  redeemed through the death of Jesus. Through the blood of
  Jesus we are delivered from our sins.

Titus and redemption

- In his letter, Titus explains that Jesus redeemed us *from*
  something and *for* something.
  "... who gave himself for us to redeem us from all
  wickedness and to purify for himself a people that are his
  very own, eager to do what is good." *Titus 2:14*
- We are redeemed *from* "all wickedness."
- We are redeemed *for* the purpose of doing "what is good."

QUOTE ABOUT
THE PASSION OF JESUS

"I will not glory because I am righteous but because I am redeemed, not because I am clear of sin, but because my sins are forgiven."
AMBROSE

PETER AND THE PASSION OF JESUS

Peter the disciple

- Impetuous Peter was the leader of Jesus' twelve disciples. He wept bitterly after denying three times that he knew Jesus. He saw Jesus die. With John, Peter was one of the first disciples to believe in Jesus' resurrection. The first Christian sermons were preached by Peter.

Peter the teacher

- The New Testament has two of Peter's letters. In his first letter we see how he explained the purpose behind Jesus' death.

QUOTE ABOUT THE PASSION OF JESUS

"When a person undergoes treatment from a doctor, he does not need to know the way in which the drug works on his body in order to be cured. There is a sense in which Christianity is like that. At the heart of Christianity there is a mystery, but it is not the mystery of intellectual appreciation; it the mystery of redemption.
WILLIAM BARCLAY

1 Jesus' death was a sacrificial death

"For you know that it was not with perishable things such as silver or gold that you were redeemed from the empty way of life handed down to you from your forefathers, but with the precious blood of Christ, a lamb without blemish or defect."
1 Peter 1:18-19

- Verse 19 is full of the language of sacrifice.

The lamb

There is the lamb. And here is no ordinary lamb, but one that was perfect for sacrifice, for it was "without blemish or defect."

The precious blood

There is the precious blood of Christ. Jesus' blood, that is his sacrificial death, is compared to the sacrifice of a lamb.

2 Jesus' death was a substitutional death

"He himself bore our sins in his body on the tree, so that we might die to sins and live for righteousness; by his wounds you have been healed."
1 Peter 2:24

- The idea of "bearing" sins is seen in Leviticus 5:17: "If a person sins and does what is forbidden in any of the LORD's commands, even though he does not know it, he is guilty and will be held responsible."

- The sins Jesus "bore" were not his own sins. He had no sins, for he was the perfect Son of God.

- The sins Jesus "bore" were "our" sins. This is how Jesus was our substitute, as he died in our place on the cross.

THE BOOK OF REVELATION AND THE PASSION OF JESUS

The Lamb in the book of Revelation

- The main way in which the book of Revelation explains the meaning of Jesus' suffering and death is through the picture of a Lamb. "Then I saw a Lamb, looking as if it had been slain, standing in the centre of the throne, encircled by the four living creatures and the elders. He had seven horns and seven eyes, which are the seven spirits of God sent out into all the earth." *Revelation 5:6*

QUOTE ABOUT THE PASSION OF JESUS

Oh! For a closer walk with God,
A calm and heavenly frame;
A light to shine upon he road
That leads to the Lamb!
So shall my walk be close
with God,
Calm and serene my frame;
So purer light shall mark the road
That leads me to the Lamb.

WILLIAM COWPER

A slain Lamb

- The Lamb in the book of Revelation was a unique Lamb. It was a "slain" Lamb. "I saw a Lamb, looking as if it had been slain."
  - This immediately recalls all the sacrificial lambs of the Old Testament sacrifices.
  - This Lamb is a name for Jesus Christ himself, and this Lamb is mentioned twenty-nine times in the book of Revelation.

A Lamb to be worshipped

- In the book of Revelation the slain Lamb is to be worshipped. "In a loud voice they sang: 'Worthy is the Lamb, who was slain, to receive power and wealth and wisdom and strength and honour and glory and praise!'" *Revelation 5:12*
- The book of Revelation concentrates on the Lamb as the heavenly Lamb, that is Jesus as he is worshipped in heaven. However, the risen Jesus is Jesus who was sacrificed. So the slain Lamb is a most appropriate picture of the work of Jesus on the cross.

Our sin and Jesus' death

- One verse in particular in the book of Revelation links the sin of humankind with Christ's work on the cross. "To him who loves us and has freed us from our sins by his blood, . . ." *Revelation 1:5*
- Here the death of Jesus, represented by his sacrificial "blood," is seen as the action that has brought us forgiveness and "has freed us from our sins."

HOW CHRISTIANS BENEFIT TODAY FROM JESUS' PASSION

Meaning and benefits

- The thirteen letters of the New Testament are crammed full of ways in which Christians today can benefit from Jesus' historic death over 2000 years ago. Note in these ten examples how everything is linked to Jesus' death.

1 The gap between us and God is removed

"But now in Christ Jesus you who once were far away have been brought near through the blood of Christ." *Ephesians 2:13*

2 We are set free from the law's curse

"Christ redeemed us from the curse of the law by becoming a curse for us, for it is written: 'Cursed is everyone who is hung on a tree.'" *Galatians 3:13*

3 We are delivered from the grip of the law

". . . having cancelled the written code, with its regulations, that was against us and that stood opposed to us; he took it away, nailing it to the cross." *Colossians 2:14*

4 We are justified before God

"Since we have now been justified by his blood, how much more shall we be saved from God's wrath through him!" *Romans 5:9*

5 We are reconciled to God

"For if, when we were God's enemies, we were reconciled to him through the death of his Son, how much more, having been reconciled, shall we be saved through his life!" *Romans 5:10*

6 We can join God's family as his children

"God sent his Son, born of a woman, born under law, to redeem those under law, that we might receive the full rights of sons."
Galatians 4:4-5

7 We can be cleansed from all sin

"But if we walk in the light, as he is in the light, we have fellowship with one another, and the blood of Jesus, his Son, purifies us from all sin." *1 John 1:7*

8 We can break the hold sin has on us

"For we know that our old self was crucified with him so that the body of sin might be rendered powerless, that we should no longer be slaves to sin – because anyone who has died has been freed from sin." *Romans 6:6-7*

9 We are no longer under God's condemnation

"Therefore, there is now no condemnation for those who are in Christ Jesus . . . For what the law was powerless to do in that it was weakened by the sinful nature, God did by sending his own Son in the likeness of sinful man to be a sin offering." *Romans 8:1-3*

10 Fear of death is taken away

"Since the children have flesh and blood, he too shared in their humanity so that by his death he might destroy him who holds the power of death – that is, the devil – and free those who all their lives were held in slavery by their fear of death."
Hebrews 2:14-15

DETAILS FROM *THE PASSION OF THE CHRIST* NOT FOUND IN THE GOSPELS

Mel Gibson's background reading

- Mel Gibson is quite open about the fact that he used sources other than the New Testament in his film: "Of course I had to study up on the crucifixion. There was this convent that was going out of business and they were selling their library. They sold them to me for a dollar a piece, so I bought 1500 of them. One of them was from Father Peter Gallwey, *The Watchers of the Sacred Passion*. It was a meditation book on the Passion of Christ. I used a lot of the book as preparation for the movie. *The Dolorous Passion of Our Lord Jesus Christ* by Saint Anne Catherine of Emmerich [an eighteenth-century Catholic mystic] was another book that just popped out at me."

Does it matter?

- The script of *The Passion of the Christ* is based primarily on New Testament accounts of the Passion, but also draws upon the above two Roman Catholic books, as well as on St. Mary of Agreda's *The Mystical City of God*.

- Many books and films give details about the life and death of Jesus that are not found in the New Testament. We may ask if this really matters? Some of these additions may seem to be of little consequence, while others may be totally heretical.

- The last chapter of the Bible warns against adding anything or taking anything away from the book of Revelation. See Revelation 22:18-19.

What about Veronica?

- Anne Catherine Emmerich, drawing on some medieval Roman Catholic mystical traditions, gives details about a woman called Veronica (the Roman Catholic Saint Veronica). In *The Passion of the Christ* Veronica is seen giving Jesus a cloth to blot, not wipe, his face on his way to his crucifixion. Legend has it that the imprint survived, and became a "relic" of the crucifixion.

- This event is not recorded by Matthew, Mark, Luke, or John.

QUOTE ABOUT
THE PASSION OF JESUS

"The Passion of the Christ *was shaped from start to finish by a devout Roman Catholic and by an almost medieval Catholic vision.*"
DAVID NEFF,
CHRISTIANITY TODAY

THE FOCUS ON PHYSICAL SUFFERING

The many physical details

- If you wanted to learn about the horrific physical details of the sufferings of Jesus, no better film has ever been made than *The Passion of the Christ*. Nobody could accuse *The Passion of the Christ* of ignoring the reason for Jesus' death. The atonement (at-one-ment), that we should be united with God, is clearly in view in the opening frame of the film with its quotations from Isaiah chapter 53.

QUOTE ABOUT THE PASSION OF JESUS

"No one who views this film's compelling imagery will ever be the same."
BILLY GRAHAM, SPEAKING ABOUT *THE PASSION OF THE CHRIST*

Why all this pain and suffering?

- The Gospels themselves state that Jesus "suffered" was "flogged," had a crown of thorns put on his head, and was crucified.

- The New Testamtent writers, writing in a time when their readers were quite familiar with the details of crucifixion, devoted more of their writing to describing the function and necessity of Jesus' death than the physical details of his crucifixion.

- In traditional Roman Catholic theology, great importance is placed on the physical sacrifice of Jesus and on preserving the memory of the details of his passion and death on the cross.

A Question for reflection

- Often times, ruminating or meditating on a question regarding the Passion can yield more understanding than looking for a quick and easy answer. As Charles Wesley, in one of his hymns, puts it: "'Tis mystery all! The Immortal dies: Who can explore this strange design?"

Atoning sacrifice

- For example, John, Jesus' closest earthly friend, explains the purpose of the cross in his first letter: "This is love: not that we loved God, but that he loved us and sent his Son as an atoning sacrifice for our sins." *1 John 4:10*

Hymns inspired by the Jesus' Passion

There is a green hill

There is a green hill far away,
Outside a city wall,
Where the dear Lord was crucified,
Who died to save us all.

O dearly, dearly, has He loved,
And we must love Him, too,
And trust in His redeeming blood,
And try His works to do.

We may not know, we cannot tell,
What pains He had to bear;
But we believe it was for us
He hung and suffered there.

He died that we might be forgiven,
He died to make us good,
That we might go at last to Heav'n,
Saved by His precious blood.

There was no other good enough
To pay the price of sin;
He only could unlock the gate
Of heaven and let us in.

O dearly, dearly has He loved,
And we must love Him, too,
And trust in His redeeming blood,
And try His works to do.

CECIL F. ALEXANDER

Story behind the hymn

• This hymn was written at the bedside of a sick child, who
  later recovered from her illness, and who always treasured it.

When I survey the wondrous cross

When I survey the wondrous cross
On which the Prince of glory died,
My richest gain I count but loss,
And pour contempt on all my pride.

Forbid it, Lord, that I should boast,
Save in the death of Christ my God!
All the vain things that charm me most,
I sacrifice them to His blood.

See from His head, His hands, His feet,
Sorrow and love flow mingled down!
Did e'er such love and sorrow meet,
Or thorns compose so rich a crown?

His dying crimson, like a robe,
Spreads o'er His body on the tree;
Then I am dead to all the globe,
And all the globe is dead to me.

Were the whole realm of nature mine,
That were a present far too small;
Love so amazing, so divine,
Demands my soul, my life, my all.
ISAAC WATTS

Story behind the hymn

- Isaac Watts first published this hymn in 1707. It was "prepared for the holy ordinance of the Lord's Supper" and headed, "Crucifixion to the world by the cross of Christ." It was inspired by Galatians 6:14, "May I never boast except in the cross of our Lord Jesus Christ, through which the world has been crucified to me, and I to the world."

QUOTE ABOUT
THE PASSION OF JESUS

"I would give up all my hymns to have written this one."
CHARLES WESLEY,
SPEAKING OF "WHEN I SURVEY THE WONDROUS CROSS"

THE WOUNDS OF JESUS

The purpose of the wounds

- Isaiah 53:5 states the meaning behind Jesus' wounds as follows:
  "But he was pierced for our transgressions,
  he was crushed for our iniquities;
  the punishment that brought us peace was upon him,
  and by his wounds we are healed."

Four types of wound

- From a medical point of view Jesus' wounds may be categorized in the following four ways.

1 The Contused wound

A contused wound results from a blow with a blunt instrument.
"They spat on him, and took the staff and struck him on the head again and again."
Matthew 27:30

2 The lacerated wound

When Jesus was flogged his flesh was torn.
"He [Pilate] had Jesus flogged." *Matthew 27:26*

QUOTE ABOUT
THE PASSION OF JESUS

"The cross of Jesus is thus the Christian symbol par excellence, forming the focal point of Christian spirituality, Christian praying, Christian believing, and Christian action. And the manifold ways in which it is and does all this can trace their roots legitimately to the mind and intention, to the action and Passion, of Jesus himself."
N. TOM WRIGHT

3 The penetrating wound

The thorns put on Jesus' head were like long, sharp, pointed instruments.
"The governor's soldiers . . . wove a crown of thorns and set it on his head." *Matthew 27:27,29*

4 The perforating wound

Iron spikes (nails) were driven into Jesus.
"... he [Thomas] declared, 'Unless I see the nail marks in his hands and put my finger where the nails were, and put my hand into his side, I will not believe it.'" *John 20:25*

JESUS DID NOT DESERVE TO SUFFER

Jesus was innocent

- Jesus was executed by the Romans as if he were a guilty common criminal. Jesus was declared innocent of any crime, on a number of occasions, by six different people.

- Jesus was declared to be innocent by:

QUOTE ABOUT
THE PASSION OF JESUS

"The Passion of the Christ *tells the story of the twelve hours surrounding the crucifixion. It is unsparing and unsentimental.*"
CHUCK COLSON

1 Judas

Judas referred to Jesus with the words "innocent blood." See Matthew 27:3-4.

2 Pilate's wife

Pilate's wife referred to Jesus as an "innocent man" in Matthew 27:19.

3 Pilate

Pilate referred to Jesus as a "this just person" in Matthew 27:24 NKJV.

Pilate said that he found no fault in Jesus in John 18:38.

4 Herod

King Herod said that Jesus had done nothing worthy of death. See Luke 23:15.

5 One of the crucified thieves

One of the thieves on the cross said that Jesus had "done nothing wrong" in Luke 23:41.

6 The centurion by the cross

After watching Jesus die, this Roman soldier concluded that Jesus was a righteous man. See Luke 23:47